THE FIRST WORLD WAR AT SEA
IN PHOTOGRAPHS

THE FIRST WORLD WAR AT SEA
IN PHOTOGRAPHS

1915

PHIL CARRADICE

AMBERLEY

Acknowledgements

My thanks go to the J&C McCutcheon Collection for providing many of the photographs seen in this book.

First published 2014

Amberley Publishing
The Hill, Stroud
Gloucestershire, GL5 4EP

www.amberley-books.com

Copyright © Phil Carradice, 2014

The right of Phil Carradice to be identified as the Author of this work has been asserted in accordance with the Copyrights, Designs and Patents Act 1988.

ISBN 978 1 4456 2237 8 (print)
ISBN 978 1 4456 2260 6 (ebook)

British Library Cataloguing in Publication Data. A catalogue record for this book is available from the British Library.

Typesetting by Amberley Publishing.
Printed in the UK.

Contents

Introduction

As far as Britain and the Royal Navy were concerned, 1914 had been a year of mixed fortunes. In just five months of war there had been many ship losses and some terrible setbacks. The sinking of the cruisers *Aboukir*, *Hogue* and *Cressy* had soon been overshadowed by disaster at the Battle of Coronel, Britain's first naval defeat for over a hundred years. The disaster had brought both the Admiralty and the whole of the British public up short, everyone suddenly realising that this was going to be no quick colonial skirmish. This was total war.

Yet there had been successes, too. The hunting down and sinking of the raider *Emden* may have taken time but it was, ultimately, a highly successful enterprise. Admiral Cradock and his men had also been avenged by the stunning and decisive victory at the Battle of the Falkland Islands, when all of von Spee's ships, apart from the light cruiser *Dresden*, had been destroyed. It meant that, in the main, 1914 ended on a relatively high note.

When they looked back over those first five months of war, the planners at the Admiralty could see that Lord Kitchener had been right when he had declared that this would be a long and bitter conflict. As Kitchener had predicted, the war had certainly not ended by Christmas and, as 1915 dawned, it brought with it further trouble.

On the very first day of the new year, the pre-Dreadnought battleship *Formidable* was torpedoed and sunk by U24 in the English Channel, almost within sight of the coast. She was not one of the newer Dreadnoughts, having been brought into service in 1904, but she was the second British capital ship to be lost in the war and, in the wake of naval losses in 1914, the effect on British morale, both in and out of the service, was devastating.

On 18 February, Germany formally announced a submarine blockade of Britain. While warships like the *Formidable* were considered fair game, previously all attacks on merchant shipping had been carried out according to the standard laws relating to war at sea. From now on, however, the war at sea would take an altogether more deadly and destructive course.

***

The naval war ran on, with highs and lows, for the rest of the year. Ships were lost, enemy ships were sunk, but there were five events or moments of particular significance for the Royal Navy. These were:

1. The Battle of the Dogger Bank
2. The running to earth and sinking of the *Dresden*, the sole German survivor of the Coronel and the Falklands Islands battles
3. The Gallipoli landings – and the eventual withdrawal of Allied troops
4. The sinking of the liner *Lusitania*
5. The destruction of the last German raider, the *Königsberg*, on the coast of Africa

The Battle of the Dogger Bank took place on 24 January when Vice Admiral David Beatty and his battlecruisers surprised Admiral Hipper and his raiding force of capital ships just off Dogger Bank.

Having already bombarded towns like Scarborough and Hartlepool the previous year, Hipper was now attempting to attack British trawlers at work on the bank, tiny ships that he and his colleagues believed were passing on information about the movements of the German battle fleet.

Thanks to the activities of Room 40 in British Naval Intelligence, radio intercepts warned the Admiralty what Hipper had in mind, and Beatty was despatched to intercept and destroy the German squadron.

As soon as he saw the smoke of the British ships, Hipper realised he was outmatched and outgunned. So he promptly wheeled around and fled back to his base. He was wise to do so. The British forces included the battlecruisers *Lion*, *Tiger*, *Princess Royal*, *New Zealand* and *Indomitable* as well as seven cruisers and thirty-five destroyers. Hipper's two scouting groups, as they were known, consisted only of the *Seydlitz*, *Moltke*, *Derfflinger* and *Blücher*, along with four cruisers and eighteen torpedo boats.

Beatty followed his adversary, and in a long and protracted stern chase the British battlecruisers gradually overhauled the enemy. What followed could have been one of the great British victories of the war but confusion over signals from the flagship caused the chase to be broken off.

Instead of destroying the badly damaged *Seydlitz* and the other fleeing vessels, all of the British ships changed course to concentrate their fire on the last ship in the German line, the *Blücher*. She was sunk, but the rest of the German squadron managed to escape, to reappear and fight again at Jutland the following year.

The cruiser *Dresden* had last been seen fleeing the carnage of the Falkland Islands, where her fast speed enabled her to show 'a clean pair of heels' to the British ships, which were low on coal and had just fought a long and bitter battle. Since then she had been hunted high and low, without success. After spending several months hiding in the fiords of South America, she was eventually run to earth on the Juan Fernández Islands on 14 March.

Despite Juan Fernández being a Chilean possession, the *Dresden* was immediately attacked.

After some token resistance, the German crew – fed up, sick at heart and totally depressed at being alone and, in their eyes at least, forgotten in the southern seas – ran up a white flag and dived over the side or took to their boats. For several minutes the men on the British ships stood and stared at this elusive quarry, which had been their target for so long.

Then the roar of explosive charges laid by the German crew against the side of the ship suddenly broke the quiet of the South American air, and the *Dresden* began to settle, bow first, in the shallow water of the bay. Finally, she turned on to her side and sank. The long chase was over.

The Cunard liner *Lusitania* was torpedoed and sunk by the U20 on the afternoon of 7 May. She was carrying 1,959 passengers and crew, many of them Americans and, therefore, technically neutral. Unfortunately, Germany had just declared all of the seas around the British coast to be a war zone, which meant that any vessel spotted by a U-boat was liable to attack.

The torpedo struck the *Lusitania* on her starboard bow, beneath the wheelhouse. Within moments there was a second explosion, within the hull of the ship – a fact later used to excuse the sinking of an unarmed merchant ship – seeming to indicate that munitions were also being carried on board. In the event the *Lusitania* sank in just eighteen minutes, taking 1,195 people down with her. Included in the dead were 128 Americans.

The sinking of the *Lusitania* caused outrage in Britain and the USA, and the propaganda machinery of both nations was wheeled out in force. America came close to declaring war on Germany over the affair and Germany was forced to issue a statement that, in future, such attacks would only be carried out on ships that could be positively identified as British.

More than anything, the sinking of the *Lusitania* demonstrated the ruthlessness of the German war machine. Equally clearly, it showed the dangers of travelling at sea, either as a neutral or as a belligerent, in time of war.

The landings at Gallipoli – the Dardanelles Campaign, to give it the correct name – were a brilliant concept that could, had they been handled correctly, have ended the war in 1915. Unfortunately, they were so badly organised and executed that they resulted only in massive casualties and, ultimately, defeat on an enormous scale.

It was the plan of Winston Churchill, First Lord of the Admiralty – a far-sighted and impressive plan, it must be admitted – to free the Dardanelles Straits for Allied shipping, to destroy Turkey's power and potential in the Middle East and, eventually, to attack Austria from the rear.

To begin with, Churchill was convinced that the narrow entrance to the Dardanelles – which was protected by a series of powerful forts and gun batteries – could be forced by the Navy. In a bombardment on 25 February, the *Queen Elizabeth* and other battleships managed to destroy the outer forts, and a body of marines and sailors stormed ashore to 'mop up' the defenders. The attack was so successful that, had they been allowed to continue, it is more than likely that the naval forces could have reached Istanbul within a few weeks and taken Turkey out of the war.

In the event, the Naval Brigade was withdrawn and the success was not followed up. It was the same story a month later when the inner forts were again shelled by British and French ships. This time minefields caused serious problems for the Navy, the ships were withdrawn and everyone settled down to wait once again.

It was a further two months before the full attack by British, Australian and New Zealand troops was finally made on the Gallipoli Peninsula. By then the Turks were fully aware of what was coming.

When, that April, the landings were made at Kum Kale, Anzac Cove and Cape Helles, ships from the Royal Navy towed the troops ashore, packed together like sardines into jolly boats and long boats, into a hail of fire from the Turkish defenders. From there things went from bad to worse. The landing forces were simply unable to get off the beaches, where the men were pinned down and gradually killed off either by enemy fire or, as the months went past, by disease.

Part of the problem was poor management and leadership of the land forces but there was also a serious flaw in the refusal of the Admiralty to accept and introduce a computerised system of range finding for the guns of their big warships.

The Royal Navy undoubtedly had the firepower to destroy the Turkish land batteries and the forts where the enemy soldiers lived, but the obsolete method of range finding used on the ships meant that their fire was largely ineffective. The Turkish guns were not destroyed and, as a result, the minefields that had been so expertly laid now waited, under the protection of the Turkish gunners, still unswept.

The battles at Gallipoli went on for many months, before, at the end of the year, the decision was made to evacuate the Gallipoli Peninsula. The evacuation began on 16 December and was largely completed by the end of the month.

Taking off the troops was carried out by the Navy with great success, so much so that the Turks did not know the soldiers had gone until it was far too late for them to interfere. If such enterprise and efficiency had been employed during the rest of the campaign the end result would have been very different.

The cruiser *Königsberg* was the last of the German surface raiders, ships that had been sent out, before war was declared, to harry and destroy Allied merchant shipping. All of the others – the *Emden*, *Karlsruhe*, every single one of von Spee's squadron – had long been sunk by the spring of 1915.

Never particularly successful as a raider – she managed to sink just one merchant vessel and an old, obsolete British cruiser – the *Königsberg*'s real value to Germany lay in the threat of her presence on the coast of Africa. It meant that troop convoys always had to be wary and the British were forced to keep ships in the area, simply patrolling and searching for the *Königsberg*.

Located and then blockaded into the Rufiji Delta on the east coast of Africa, the end of the *Königsberg* came on 15 July. Despite edging further and further upstream, and despite camouflaging her decks with trees from the bank, the German ship simply had nowhere to go.

In what was an early example of cooperation between aircraft and ships, the *Königsberg* was battered by shells from the shallow draught monitors *Severn* and *Mersey*. The monitors' fire was spotted and directed by two aeroplanes, and although one was hit by fire from the cruiser, the other managed to relay exact location and fall of shot to the monitors. In little over an hour the *Königsberg* had been sunk.

* * *

Other moments of note during 1915 included the sinking of several British warships, battleships in particular, during the Gallipoli campaign. There were also increasingly successful submarine patrols by both British and German boats and the first use of Q-ships, decoy vessels designed to lure U-boats to the surface where they could be destroyed by gunfire.

On 17 May Jacky Fisher, the First Sea Lord, walked out of the Admiralty after a row with his chief, Winston Churchill. Supremely confident and self-opinionated, Fisher wrote a letter to Herbert Asquith, the Prime Minister, detailing his demands and outlining exactly what he needed to be put in place before he would even contemplate returning to the Admiralty.

Fisher then set off for his home in Scotland, confidently expecting to hear a grovelling capitulation from Asquith within a day or so. On the platform of Crewe station he was met by the stationmaster with a telegram. Asquith had accepted his resignation. Meekly and with his bluff called, Jacky Fisher retired from public life.

The first British success against a Zeppelin occurred on 7 June when Sub-Lt Warneford of the Royal Naval Air Service dropped a bomb onto the fuselage of LZ37, and watched in a combination of horror and glee as the giant airship exploded. Warneford's action gained for him and the RNAS their first Victoria Cross of the war. It was an award given directly by the king and was granted within a week of the event taking place.

The year ended, as normal, it seemed to those in the know, with disaster. On 31 December, New Year's Eve, the armoured cruiser *Natal* was taking on ammunition when she suddenly blew up in the Cromarty Firth. Over 400 men died in the explosion, along with ten civilians who were on board for lunch and a celebratory film show.

January

H.M.S. FORMIDABLE PASSING THE KING JULY 20ᵀᴴ 1914.

The battleship HMS *Formidable* was torpedoed and sunk on New Year's Day 1915. On 31 December, along with the rest of the 5th Battle Squadron, she had been involved in exercises in the English Channel, and, despite reports of U-boat activity in the area, remained at sea all night. With the sea rough and the wind rising it was felt that the chances of a U-boat attack were slim. Off Portland Bill, steaming at 12 knots at the rear of the squadron, at 02.20 in the morning *Formidable* was struck by a torpedo fired from U24. At 3.05 she was struck by a second torpedo and an hour and a half later rolled over onto her side and sank.

Captain Noel Loxley remained on board the *Formidable* to the end, standing on the bridge with his fox terrier Bruce as the ship went down. The body of the faithful dog was later washed up on the coast and buried in Dorset. Out of a complement of 780 sailors, 35 officers and 512 men were drowned. A well-recounted story, also about an animal and the disaster, concerns the dog belonging to the Pilot Boat Inn in Lyme Regis, which was being used as a temporary mortuary. The dog apparently licked the face of a supposedly dead sailor, Able Seaman John Cowan, and brought him back to life. According to legend, the film moguls of Hollywood heard the story and used it as the basis for the series of Lassie films.

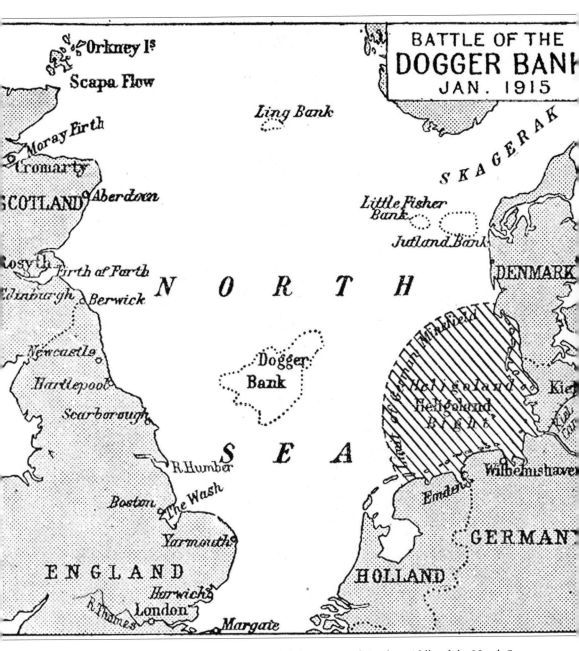

Dogger Bank, the enormous and well-stocked fishing grounds in the middle of the North Sea, was the scene of the first big gun encounter of the war when the battlecruisers of admirals Beatty and Hipper clashed on 24 January. This map shows the location of the battle.

GREAT BRITISH NAVAL VICTORY IN THE NORTH SEA. THE FIRST BATTLE BETWEEN DREADNOUGHTS. JAN. 24 TH
INDOMITABLE. NEW ZEALAND. PRINCESS ROYAL. UNDAUNTED. TIGER. AURORA. LION (FLAGSHIP). ARETHUSA. BLUCHER. DERFFINGER. SEYDLITZ. MOLTK
THIRD DESTROYER FLOTILLA.   FIRST DESTROYER FLOTILLA.

The Battle of Dogger Bank, an artist's impression. Hipper was intending to attack British trawlers fishing on the bank but Beatty, alerted to his intentions, intercepted with a more powerful force. In a running fight, ships of both sides suffered severe damage. HMS *Lion* was so badly damaged that she had to drop out of the line while Hipper's *Seydlitz* was lucky to escape and limp back to port.

Opposite top: With the *Lion* out of action, Beatty was forced to transfer his flag, firstly to the destroyer *Attack* which came up alongside the battered battlecruiser and took him off, and then to the battlecruiser *Princess Royal*. This shows the admiral commanding operations from the canvas bridge of the *Attack* while waiting to be transferred to the *Princess Royal*.

Opposite bottom: David Beatty on the *Attack*. Legend states that as he came aboard a sailor slapped him on the back and declared, 'Well done, David, you're the man to thrash these Germans.' Beatty would have agreed with the sentiment but it is hardly likely that the autocratic admiral would have allowed a common sailor to come close, let alone touch him.

AFTER HIS FLAG-SHIP THE "LION" HAD BEEN HIT: ADMIRAL SIR DAVID BEATTY, ON THE BRIDGE OF THE DESTROYER "ATTACK," APPROACHING THE "PRINCESS ROYAL" TO HOIST HIS FLAG

ADMIRAL SIR DAVID BEATTY

H.M.S. LION.

Admiral Beatty (inset) and his powerful flagship HMS *Lion*. Battlecruisers – fast, well armed but lightly armoured – were the symbol of British power, the romantic ships of the Navy, and suited Beatty's temperament perfectly.

The *Lion* was so badly damaged in the battle that she had to be towed back home. This shows the *Indomitable* taking her in tow for the long haul back to port. Escorting destroyers can be seen in the background.

Hipper's flagship, the battlecruiser *Seydlitz*. Like *Lion* she suffered serious damage during the battle and was only saved from an internal explosion when an alert sailor flooded the magazines to prevent fire spreading. In the wake of the battle the Germans realised not only the flaws in the ammunition-handling and storing procedures on their ships, but also their weak magazine protection, and took steps to improve these. The British did not.

Above: Left to the tender mercies of the whole battlecruiser fleet, the *Blücher* was soon despatched. Hipper, on the *Seydlitz*, had no choice – he could not help his disabled colleague and he had to save the rest of the fleet. As shells rained in on the *Blücher*, she turned onto her side; men slid down the shattered hull and she sank slowly below the waves.

Opposite top: The *Blücher* was the oldest ship in the German squadron, having been completed in 1909. The rear ship in the German line, she was outgunned and outclassed by the British battlecruisers, and was soon disabled.

Opposite bottom: An artist's impression of the sinking of the *Blücher*. Her sinking inadvertently saved the *Seydlitz* and the other German ships. Having been forced to leave the crippled *Lion*, Beatty made two signals – 'Engage the enemy's rear' and 'Course NE'. He meant that they should attack the rear of the fleeing German fleet (the NE signal was just to limit the degree of turn his ships should make) but, as both signals were flown on the same hoist, his second-in-command, Rear Admiral Gordon Moore, on the *New Zealand* assumed Beatty meant that the rear ship, the *Blücher*, should be finished off. As a consequence he broke off the action against the other German ships to concentrate on the *Blücher*.

Admiral Franz von Hipper (centre) with his staff. Interestingly, the future commander of the German navy in the Second World War, Admiral Raeder – then still a fairly junior officer – stands second from the left in the photograph.

Opposite top: HMS *Arethusa*, one of seven British cruisers present at the battle, sends out her boats to rescue the crew of the *Blücher*.

Opposite bottom: Admiral Beatty and his staff pose on the deck of HMS *Lion*.

The Captain of the *Blücher* was saved from his sinking ship but died soon afterwards. This shows his funeral cortège as he is buried with full military honours.

HMS *Repulse* was originally intended to be an improved version of the Revenge Class of battleship, but work was suspended on her when war broke out. Jacky Fisher ordered her construction to be restarted on 25 January, the day after the Battle of Dogger Bank. She was now to be a battlecruiser, and the builders promised to deliver her in just fifteen months.

This shows the *Renown*, sister ship to the *Repulse*. Her building was restarted the same day, the same claims being made by the builders because battlecruisers did not require the same amount of protection as battleships. In both cases the builders were out in their calculations by a few months, both *Renown* and *Repulse* being delivered shortly after Jutland in 1916.

The *Queen Elizabeth*, completed in January 1915, was one of the finest battleships ever built. She is shown here after conversion work, with her two funnels trunked into one. Armed with eight 15-inch guns, plus a smaller secondary armament, she was a powerful weapon of war. Her extra 4 knots of speed enabled her to work easily and efficiently with the battlecruiser squadrons.

February

Coaling, the most hated task in the Navy. Thousands of tons of best Welsh anthracite were used by the Royal Navy, all of it having to be slung on board and manhandled into the bunkers. As the war progressed, however, the Royal Navy moved more and more to oil firing – much to the delight of the sailors. On battleships such as the *Queen Elizabeth* and *Warspite*, coal was only used for auxiliary purposes.

On 18 February Germany began a submarine blockade of Britain. In future any merchant ships carrying goods to British ports would be sunk without warning.

The Cabinet had given its approval to Churchill's proposal for an attack on the Dardanelles on 28 January. On 25 February a combined French-British fleet moved into position, and the first bombardment of the outer forts protecting the Dardanelles Straits took place. The bombardment was hugely successful and was followed up by landings of troops from the Royal Naval Division.

The massive 15-inch guns of the *Queen Elizabeth* are seen in this photograph. The bombardment of the outer forts was the first time the *Queen Elizabeth*, then the most powerful battleship in the world, had been in action. Her guns pummelled the Turkish positions but, despite the success, the assault petered out and the golden chance of a breakthrough was lost.

Opposite top: The 13.5-inch guns of the *Iron Duke* are shown here, being fired in practice. The amount of smoke invariably caused problems for gun setters and those who gauged the fall of shot.

Opposite bottom: A squadron of German Dreadnought battleships heads out to sea, complete with watching Zeppelin overhead.

March

Submarine warfare intensified at the beginning of March. On the 11th of the month the armed merchant cruiser *Bayono*, en route from Glasgow to Liverpool, was torpedoed and sunk by U27 10 miles off Carswell Point in Scotland. No warning was given, the ship sank quickly and 195 officers and crew were drowned before they could take to the boats.

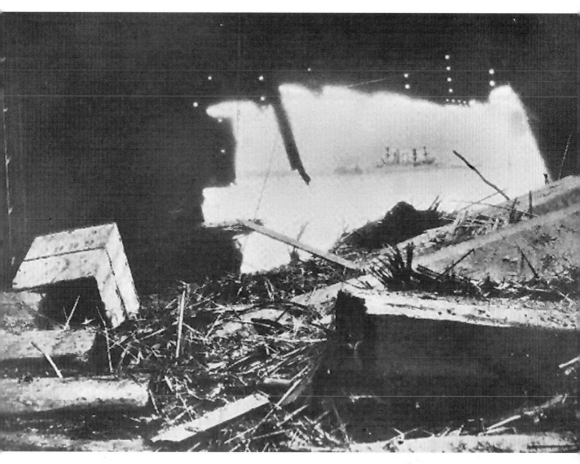

The effect of a torpedo strike was usually immense, often fatal, for the stricken ship. This shows the hole blown in the side of one ship that has received a hit from an enemy torpedo, the photograph being taken from inside the vessel.

Above: Tracking down and destroying the *Dresden*, the sole German survivor of the Falklands Islands battle, became a matter of honour for the men of the Royal Navy. The search was left in the hands of Admiral Stoddart, with vessels like the *Glasgow*, *Kent* and *Orama* being the main hunters. Captain Ludecke of the *Dresden* took his ship into Christmas Bay on the rugged Chilean coast, where she saw in New Year 1915 surrounded by snow-capped mountains.

Opposite page: On the afternoon of 5 March, the U8 was surprised by a flotilla of destroyers off Dover. Brought to the surface, the German crew were taken off their sinking vessel, many of them stepping into boats of the British destroyers without getting their feet wet. The prisoners were then taken in to Dover, the first German sailors the townsfolk had seen.

Above: The *Dresden* could not hide forever, and on Sunday 14 March she was spotted by the cruiser *Kent*, at anchor in Cumberland Bay on the island of Juan Fernández (opposite). Despite Chilean waters being neutral, the *Kent*, *Glasgow* and *Orama* entered the bay and opened fire. The *Dresden* fired a few rounds in reply, then hoisted a white flag. The crew swam or took boats to the shore. In 1909, she had visited New York for the Hudson-Fulton celebrations, where she is seen in this photograph.

Opposite top: Raising a white flag had been a ruse to give the German crew time to set explosive charges against the *Dresden*'s hull. These soon exploded and the ship sank, slowly at first, then quite rapidly. British sailors landed to give first aid to wounded Germans, who were then taken to hospital in Valparaiso. This shows the *Dresden* moments before she sank.

Opposite bottom: A close-up view showing the port side of the ship and the damage that the British shells and the charges had caused to the hull of the *Dresden*.

Above: Karl Dönitz, later commander of the U-boat arm of the German Navy in the Second World War, served on board the cruiser *Breslau*, which, along with the *Goeben*, successfully ran the British blockade in the Mediterranean in 1914. During 1915, with the *Breslau* now in the Turkish Navy, he was active in the Turkish campaigns against the Russians in the Black Sea.

Opposite top: The U29, under the command of Otto Weddigen, is shown here on a German postcard, leaving port for her last cruise. A few days later she was cut in half by the battleship *Dreadnought* when, having fired torpedoes at the *Neptune*, she unluckily broke the surface directly in the path of the British battleship. There were no survivors.

Opposite bottom: The battleship *Dreadnought* had been a revolutionary vessel when she was launched in 1906 but by the start of the war she was already outdated. Despite this, in 1914 she was flagship of the 4th Battle Squadron, and on 18 March 1915 she rammed and sank the U29 in the Pentland Firth. The U29 was the command of Otto Weddigen, the first U-boat ace of the war and the man who, when he was captain of the U9, had sunk the *Aboukir*, *Hogue* and *Cressy*.

Kapitänleutnant **Weddigen,**
ehemaliger
Kommandant der Unterseeboote
U 9. und U 29.

A German memorial card for Otto Weddigen. For the first few months of the war, Weddigen had lived a charmed life. As well as sinking the three British cruisers in September 1914, he also accounted for HMS *Hawk* and several merchantmen. He was awarded the Iron Cross and the Pour le Mérite before his transfer to the U29 and his death on 18 March.

On 18 March, during a naval assault on the forts of the Dardanelles, the French pre-Dreadnought *Bouvet* was sunk with the loss of over 650 lives. She had been hit eight times by shells from the land batteries, then ran into a minefield and sank in just two minutes. The British battleships *Irresistible* and *Ocean* were sunk during the same operation.

The *Ocean*, sunk in the Dardanelles in March 1915. The loss of three capital ships caused the planners to call off the naval attacks and concentrate on land assaults instead.

The destroyer *Dasher*, one of the original 'turtle backs' that, despite their ungainly appearance, managed a top speed of 27 knots.

April

Sailors working on a contact mine. Along with torpedoes, mines were perhaps the most deadly weapon of the sea war, accounting for dozens of victims on both sides of the conflict.

By 3 April 1915 the Dover Straits mine barrage was completed and in place. This shows a British minelayer dropping mines over the stern of the ship as the crew prepares the next weapon and watches the mines bob away.

RUPERT BROOKE WRITING IN GARDEN
OF THE OLD VICARAGE, GRANTCHESTER.

The poet Rupert Brooke had already achieved immortality with his poem 'The Soldier' and its lines 'If I should die think only this of me/That there's some corner of a foreign field/That is forever England' when he and the rest of the Hood Battalion of the Royal Naval Division were detailed to take part in the forthcoming Gallipoli campaign. Brooke was destined never to reach the Dardanelles but died en route, from septicaemia caused by an infected mosquito bite. This shows the poet in the garden of his house at Granchester outside Cambridge.

Above: Rupert Brooke and the rest of the officers of the Hood Battalion at Blandford Camp in Dorset, in around February 1915, just prior to their departure for the Dardanelles. Having died on the way to the Dardanelles, Rupert Brooke was buried in a quiet and secluded grove on the Mediterranean island of Scyros.

Right: A Royal Naval Division badge, the crossed machine guns indicating that this was the emblem of a machine-gun company.

British troops going ashore at the Dardanelles. The original assault had been planned for 23 April, but was delayed because of bad weather, and as a result the attack began on 25 April. From the beginning things went badly wrong. Even on W Beach, where the Lancashire Regiment made their assault and overwhelmed the defenders, there were still 600 casualties. On V Beach the casualty figure was as high as 70 per cent.

Australian and New Zealand troops landing at Anzac Cove. The name Anzac (the Australian and New Zealand Army Corps) became a byword for courage and bravery during the course of the Gallipoli campaign. Most Anzacs were, however, hugely critical of the leadership displayed by British officers.

SOUTH AFRICA   AUSTRALIA   CANADA   NEW ZEALAND   INDIA

ONE KING   ONE FLAG   ONE EMPIRE

'One King, One Flag, One Empire,' the caption to this patriotic postcard reads. Most Anzac soldiers, as they sweated in the heat and cursed the flies that swarmed around the bloated corpses of their comrades, would have had some difficulty believing the sentiment.

Above: Barbed-wire entanglements, laid by the Turks as they waited for the assaults to begin. The value of barbed wire had already been shown on the battlefields of France and, as yet, no one had found a way to cut or destroy it. This photograph also shows the armada of Allied warships waiting just off the coast.

Opposite top: Troops being taken ashore. There were no landing craft or specialised vessels for the landings, just hastily gathered ships' boats, usually commanded by a midshipman and crewed by half a dozen unhappy sailors.

Opposite bottom: Pre-Dreadnought battleships entering the Dardanelles to support the Allied landings on the Gallipoli Peninsula. Despite regular naval barrages, troops never really managed to get far beyond the landing beaches. The one time when a unit of Ghurkhas did manage to fight their way off the beach and climb to the top of a ridge overlooking Suvla Bay, gunners on the ships offshore were convinced that no Allied unit could have penetrated that far inland and opened fire on them. The Ghurkhas were forced to retreat to the beach.

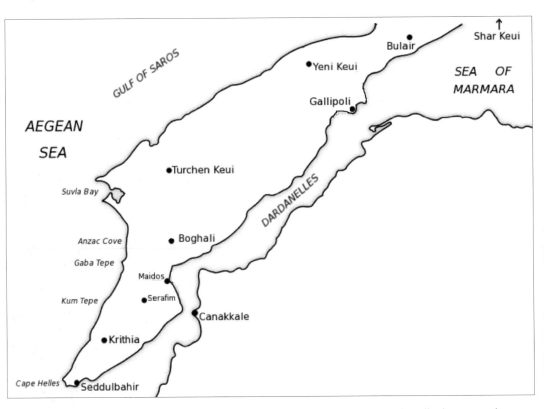

A map of the Gallipoli Peninsula, showing the various landing beaches. The Allied commander, Sir Ian Hamilton, was a kindly, good-natured man, totally unsuited to the task of managing amphibious landings and conducting a sustained campaign against a determined enemy. He spent most of the time cruising up and down the coast, sailing between one landing beach and another, totally out of touch with the reality of the situation.

The landing beach at Seddil Bahr, a photograph taken from the steamer *River Clyde*. It shows horses, guns and provisions going ashore – all under fire from the Turkish guns. The beach and the water offshore are a hive of activity, but organisation seems to be missing.

Right: A cigarette card showing Captain Unwin of the *River Clyde*. Things did not go to plan, and no sooner had the lighters been positioned beside the *River Clyde* than they were swept away by the tide. Captain Unwin and Able Seaman Williams dived over the side and, under heavy enemy fire, manhandled two lighters into position. Williams was killed, but Unwin, despite being wounded, held his position. He later rescued several wounded men from the beach and was awarded the Victoria Cross for his bravery.

Opposite top: The *River Clyde*, a 4,000-ton collier, was converted into what was euphemistically known as a landing ship. Doorways were cut into her side and the idea was for troops to disembark onto bridges made out of smaller craft and from there on to land. On 15 April she was run ashore on V Beach.

Opposite bottom: Transports disembarking troops at one of the Gallipoli beaches, despite being under fire from the Turkish batteries.

The plan was for the *River Clyde* to remain on the beach so that troops could be ferried on board, using the ship as cover, then disembark directly onto shore. This shows her after she was grounded as a landing stage on V Beach.

Edward Courtney Beale is shown here on the deck of his submarine E14. On 27 April Beale took the E14 into the Sea of Marmara, diving under the minefields, and began operations in the narrow waters. He sank two gunboats and a large Turkish transport and, as a result, was awarded the Victoria Cross.

May

On 1 May 1915 the US merchant ship *Gulflight* was torpedoed and sunk by U30 off the Scilly Isles. No warning was given. The *Gulflight* was the first American merchant ship to be lost in the war.

On 13 May the battleship *Goliath* was sunk in Morto Bay, Cape Helles. She was hit by torpedoes fired from the destroyer *Muavenet I Milliye*, a Turkish vessel manned by a combined Turkish and German crew. The *Goliath* sank quickly, taking 570 of her crew down with her, including Captain Shelford.

On 17 May, after a row with Churchill, Jacky Fisher walked out of his post as First Sea Lord at the Admiralty. Believing he was indispensable, he expected to be recalled within a few days, but it did not happen and he retired into an unhappy and embittered old age. He died in 1920. Fisher and Winston Churchill are seen here in happier times.

This and previous page: Yet another British pre-Dreadnought went to the bottom on 25 May when the *Triumph* was torpedoed by U21 off Cape Tepe outside the Dardanelles. The torpedo tore through the battleship's guarding torpedo nets before exploding on the ship's starboard quarter. Destroyers came alongside and managed to take off most of the crew, with the result that only seventy-eight men were killed.

Lieut.-Comm. M. E. NASMITH, V.C.

Above: On 20 May Martin Nasmith took the E11 through the Dardanelles into the Sea of Marmara. During the next few weeks he sank a Turkish gunboat, two large transports, an ammunition ship and, just before he returned from the patrol, a large coal ship as she was coming in to dock. This shows the triumphant Nasmith and his crew on the deck of the E11.

Left: A cigarette card showing a head-and-shoulders view of Martin Nasmith. For his efforts in the Sea of Marmara, Nasmith was awarded the Victoria Cross, and several of his crew also received decorations.

German Transport sunk by a British Submarine in the sea of Marmora on June 3rd 1915.

A postcard view showing the destruction of a German transport in the Sea of Marmara. Although they are not named, in all probability this was the work of Nasmith and the E11.

The submarine E11, perhaps the most famous and certainly the most successful British submarine of the First World War.

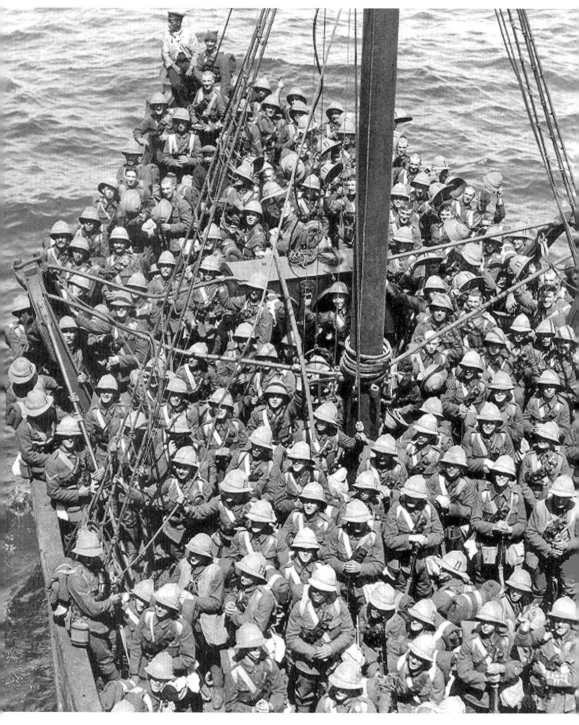

Reinforcements were often required throughout the Gallipoli campaign. This shows the
Lancashire Fusiliers landing on W Beach in May 1915.

A casualty clearing station at Gallipoli. The place was probably cleaned up for the photograph – the reality would have been far more unpleasant, with wounded sailors and soldiers arriving at every moment of the day.

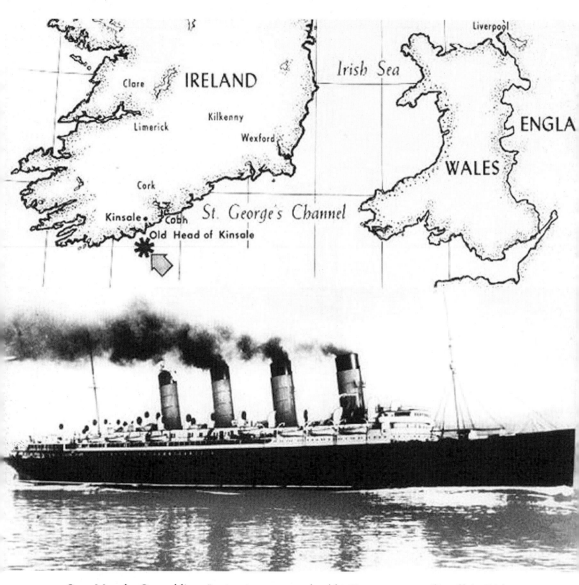

On 7 May the Cunard liner *Lusitania* was torpedoed by U20 some 11 miles off the Irish coast. She had left America on the 1st of the month and was now approaching Liverpool, her journey's end. She carried 1,198 passengers and crew, many of them American citizens. This postcard from the time shows the ship and the spot where she was sunk.

The following images are artist-drawn impressions of the Gallipoli landings and the Dardanelles campaign. All are courtesy of the J&C McCutcheon Collection.

The *Lusitania* was one of the most luxurious ships of her day. A previous holder of the Blue Riband for the fastest crossing of the Atlantic, she was capable of making 25 knots. Unfortunately, Germany had just declared the seas around Britain a war zone – all ships encountered in the zone were therefore likely or possible targets. The German Embassy in Washington DC had actually placed an advertisement in the press, advising people not to travel on the *Lusitania*, but the warning went largely unheeded.

The final plunge, an artist-drawn card showing the end of the *Lusitania*. Only six of the liner's forty-eight lifeboats were launched before she went to the bottom and, out of a total of 1,959 passengers and crew, 1,195 lost their lives. In a tragic replaying of the *Titanic* disaster of 1912, the *Lusitania* went down by the bows, stern high up in the air, and most of the casualties died, as the passengers from the *Titanic* had died, from hypothermia.

Opposite top: The *Lusitania* was due to dock in Liverpool late in the afternoon of 7 May. It was sheer chance that she and the U20 should meet as there was no way the slower submarine could have intercepted or kept up with the liner.

Opposite bottom: An imaginative German postcard showing the single torpedo fired by Captain Schwieger of the U20 striking the *Lusitania* on the starboard bow. Within moments of the torpedo striking, there was a second explosion, from deep inside the hull of the liner. This, said the Germans, was proof that the *Lusitania* was carrying munitions, something that made her a legitimate target of war. Recent revelations would seem to indicate that the liner was, indeed, carrying somewhere in the region of 50 tonnes of 3-inch shells.

The sinking of the 'Lusitania'-1915

A painting showing the end of the *Lusitania*. The sinking caused outrage, both in Britain and America – 128 of the dead were Americans – and for a while there was a possibility that the USA could declare war on Germany. It did not happen, but Germany was forced to abandon its 'sink on sight' policy. It was two years later, in January 1917, before unrestricted submarine warfare was reintroduced.

Opposite top: Bodies were washed ashore on the Irish coast for several weeks after the sinking. This shows the funeral of some of the *Lusitania* victims. Propaganda from both sides in the conflict made the most of the disaster, but the long-held belief that German schoolchildren were given a day's holiday to celebrate the sinking has little or no credibility.

Opposite bottom: Retribution? This shows the end of U20, the submarine that sank the *Lusitania*. After damage to her engines, on 4 November 1916 the U20 was washed up on the Danish coast near Vrist. The crew detonated torpedoes inside her hull to destroy the U-boat, and the Danish Navy later cut holes in her side to ensure she could never be used again.

Men of the Royal Naval Division charging the Turks during the Gallipoli campaign.

Sir Ian Hamilton, the man in charge of the landings and the campaign, spends a rare few hours ashore. He is seen here during an inspection of his troops.

On 27 May, the Allied forces lost their third capital ship in two weeks when the *Majestic* was torpedoed by U21. The battleship had been exchanging fire with shore batteries but, when struck by the torpedo, took only nine minutes to capsize and sink below the waves. This view of her sinking was taken from another Royal Navy ship.

Above: Another view of the end
of the battleship *Majestic*, this one
taken moments before she turned
turtle and sank.

Right: Jacky Fisher might have
expected to be quickly recalled after
walking out of the Admiralty – he
genuinely believed that there was
no one else who could do the job of
First Sea Lord as well as him – but,
as it happened, Churchill soon
found a replacement. Admiral Sir
Henry Jackson was appointed First
Sea Lord on 28 May 1915.

Destroyers patrolling in the North Sea, a drawing by marine artist W. L. Wyllie.

June

British battleships off Gallipoli. Included in their number is the new *Queen Elizabeth*, although the men at the Admiralty soon ran scared and withdrew her. Ship-to-ship combat was one thing, but it would not do to have the most powerful ship in the world damaged or sunk by Turkish mines, shore batteries or torpedoes.

Soldiers bathing off one of the Gallipoli beaches, a rare moment of relief from the agony they had to endure in their daily lives. Such pleasures as sea bathing at least enabled men to get clean, but the activity was invariably carried out under Turkish fire.

On 7 June, Flight Sub-Lt Reginald Warneford of the Royal Naval Air Service became the first man to bring down a Zeppelin. The giant German airships had been terrorising mainland Britain, attacking and dropping bombs, seemingly at will, for some time. Warneford's victory over LZ37 took place over Ghent as she was returning to base.

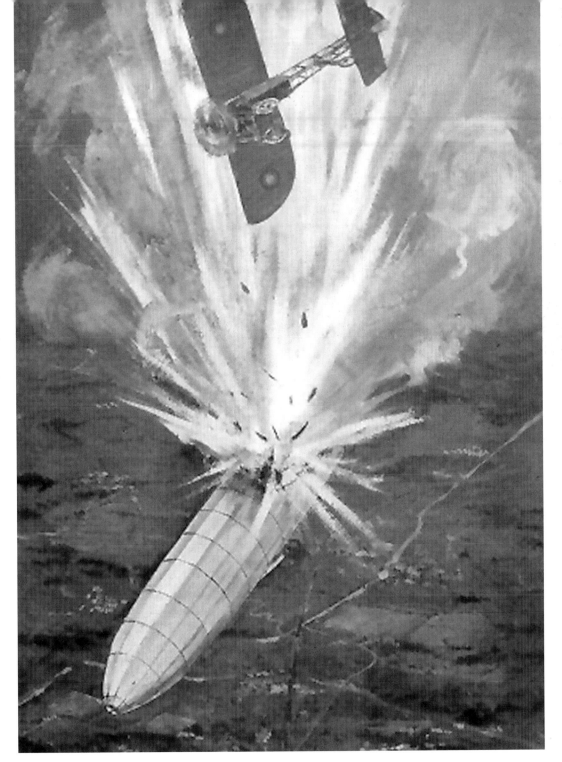

Warneford destroyed his airship by dropping bombs onto it. The blast turned his Morane Saulnier Scout upside down and stopped the engine – Warneford had to land behind German lines for emergency repairs before taking off again and returning to his base. Awarded the VC for his actions, Warneford died in an accident just two weeks after his victory.

With the need to build and repair ships remaining strong, the new facility of Rosyth dockyard in Scotland was opened by the king on 8 June. This view shows the battlecruiser *Tiger* in dry dock at the new dockyard.

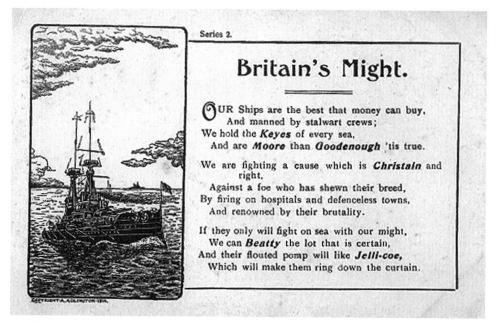

Series 2.

Britain's Might.

OUR Ships are the best that money can buy,
 And manned by stalwart crews;
We hold the *Keyes* of every sea,
 And are *Moore* than *Goodenough* 'tis true.

We are fighting a cause which is *Christain* and
 right,
 Against a foe who has shewn their breed,
By firing on hospitals and defenceless towns,
 And renowned by their brutality.

If they only will fight on sea with our might,
 We can *Beatty* the lot that is certain,
And their flouted pomp will like *Jelli-coe*,
 Which will make them ring down the curtain.

Britain's Might, a poem card that manages to include the names of several well-known admirals, Jellicoe and Beatty among them.

Throughout the summer of 1915 the battles and skirmishes on the Gallipoli Peninsula continued. This shows British artillery, landed to give extra weight to the daily bombardment of Turkish positions by the Navy.

Casualties remained high throughout the Gallipoli campaign. With reinforcements constantly being sent, nearly half a million Allied troops fought on the peninsula, 250,000 of them becoming casualties. Disease was as much a killer as Turkish shells and bullets. Ferrying the wounded off the beaches, as this photograph shows, soon became one of the major tasks of the Navy.

July

End of Königsberg in the Rufiji Delta
W L Wyllie.

On 15 July the raider *Königsberg* was finally destroyed when the flat-bottomed monitors *Mersey* and *Severn* managed to steam far enough up the Rufiji Delta to shell her. Two spotter aircraft were used to direct the fire of the monitors, the first time effective sea-air cooperation was used in the war.

A potentially powerful and dangerous ship, the real value of the *Königsberg* lay in her threat rather than her actual guns. As long as she was free – albeit bottled up in an African river – the Royal Navy had to deploy ships to keep watch in case she tried to escape. When she was finally destroyed, her remains slowly sinking into the mud of the delta, it was a great relief to Churchill and the men at the Admiralty.

The *Severn*, shown here, was one of three shallow-draught monitors originally built for the Brazilian navy and taken over by the British early on in the war. Armed with 6-inch guns, the *Severn*, *Mersey* and *Humber* were relatively small and light vessels – their weapons could certainly not compete with the enormous 12-inch and 14-inch guns of later monitors. Nevertheless, with their fall of shot corrected by naval aircraft, they were hugely effective against the *Königsberg*.

The remains of the German raider *Königsberg*, shown here in the shallow waters of the Rufiji Delta. If the British had only known it, the cruiser was ineffective and immobilised because of serious damage to her engines, parts of which had already been sent overland for repair in one of the German colonies.

The idea behind Q-ships, decoy vessels that did not seem worth a torpedo and would, therefore, lure U-boats to the surface where they would be attacked by gunfire, began in the summer of 1915. This view shows the Q-ship *Privet*. Her guns are hidden, and any U-boat watching the ship through its periscope would think her a harmless victim. Some Q-ships even had sailors dressed as women parading around their decks in order to convince the U-boats of their innocence.

The U36, an early victim of the Q-ships. The first successful 'decoy ship' action came on 23 June when a combined operation between the trawler *Taranaki* and the submarine C24 sank the U40 – the German captain of the U40 considered it 'a low-down trick'. The first real Q-ship success of the war came a day later when the decoy vessel *Prince Charles* lured U36 to the surface and sank her with gunfire.

Lifebelt and lifeboat drill on board a passenger liner. After the sinking of the *Lusitania*, shipping companies were wary about safety of their passengers.

British submarine successes in the Dardanelles and the Sea of Marmara were a welcome fillip for the Admiralty, but there were also losses. This shows the E7, later sunk when she became trapped in anti-submarine nets. Despite being depth charged, the E7 was eventually scuttled by her own crew.

Throughout 1915, almost until the end, reinforcements regularly made the passage by convoy from Britain to Egypt where they trained and were 'acclimatised' to the heat before setting off for Gallipoli. This shows an artillery regiment posing in front of the giant Sphinx. Within a few weeks they would be on the beaches of Gallipoli.

The crew of a British minesweeper pose in their lifebelts and safety collars. The job of the minesweeper crews was a thankless and dangerous one but it was essential if the capital ships of the Navy were to be kept safe.

Disposing of a mine the hard way. Sailors take aim at a floating mine and hope to destroy it by putting a rifle bullet on to the end of one of the contacts on the mine's skin – a keen eye and a strong nerve were required for this job.

August

A French aeroplane is shown here above an Allied squadron, about to bombard forts on the Dardanelles. The French were actively involved in the operation, but as the year wore on it seemed as if the brunt of the fighting, both at sea and on land, was borne by the British and Anzac forces.

History was made on 8 August when a Sopwith Schneider floatplane was flown off a ramp on the deck of the *Campania*, the first time that an aircraft had flown off the deck of a ship at sea. The pilot was Flight Lieutenant William Welsh. Originally a Cunard liner and holder of the Blue Riband, the *Campania* was bought by the Admiralty for use as an armed merchant cruiser at the beginning of the war. Converted into a seaplane tender, the two forward guns were removed, and a take-off ramp installed – it can be clearly seen in this photograph.

Flying aircraft off the decks of ships was not really viable at this early stage of the war, and by October the feat had been repeated only three times. In the years to come, however, it was clear that flying aircraft off the deck of a ship rather than winching them into the water for take-off was the way forward. This shows an aircraft taking off from a ramp installed over the gun barrels of the battleship *Barham* later in the war.

S. M. S. Moltke, Heckansicht.

Operating in the Gulf of Riga, the submarine E1 torpedoed the German Dreadnought *Moltke* on 19 August. It was the first time a Dreadnought – as opposed to a pre-Dreadnought – had been torpedoed. In the event the *Moltke* was badly damaged, but did not sink and was able to make it back to port.

The track of a torpedo, often the first inkling anyone might have that a ship was actually under attack.

The U29 is shown here alongside the merchant ship *Headland*. The photograph was taken by the Captain of the *Headland* ten minutes before he and his crew were ordered into the boats, after which the U29 torpedoed and sank the merchant ship.

Still the Gallipoli campaign ground on! Wounded soldiers are seen here, being taken out to waiting transports in barges.

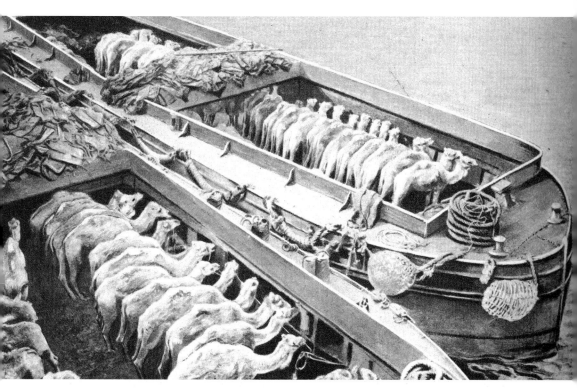

Camels being taken from Egypt for the Gallipoli campaign – quite what use they were on the narrow beaches that the soldiers never really left is not clear.

Engl. Dampfer unter amerikan. Flagge überrennt hilflose Schiff brüchige des deutschen U-Bootes „U 41" am 24. 9. 15.

The Q-ship *Baralong*, which, on 19 August, sank the U27 in the Western Approaches. This is a German drawing of the ship at work.

On 21 August the merchantman *Ruel* was sunk by the U38 just south of the Bishop Rock. The crew took to the lifeboats, where they were promptly fired on by sailors from the U38. It was the first instance of such behaviour in the war, and might well reflect German anger at the activity (and success) of the British Q-ships. This German painting shows how the Germans would have preferred their U-boat war to be recorded.

FOR KING AND COUNTRY
OUR DEFENDERS ON LAND AND SEA

A composite postcard view showing the king and British admirals and generals, with Jellicoe and Jacky Fisher among them.

September

On 24 September, the Q-ship *Baralong* recorded her second success in a month when she sank the U41 approximately 100 miles to the west of Ushant.

Lord Kitchener going on board the *Iron Duke*. Despite his belief that the war would last a long time, Kitchener became increasingly isolated and ineffective as the conflict ground on, his role and duties seeming to be restricted to visits to the front and to the ships of the Grand Fleet. By September 1915 he was really little more than a figurehead.

Rule Britannia, a jingoistic British postcard sent in 1915.

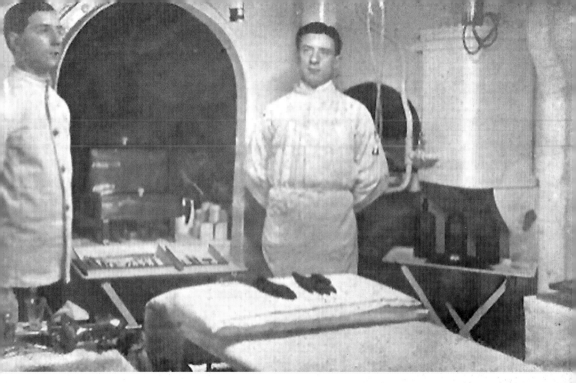

A surgery and sickbay on board a British battleship. The longer the war went on, the more facilities for immediate first aid and medical help became increasingly vital, particularly in far-flung parts of the world.

This photograph shows the *Thordis*, reportedly the first British merchant ship to sink an enemy submarine. The U-boat was rammed off Beachy Head and the merchantman limped home – however, there appears to be very little damage to the bows of the ship in this view.

Supplies of bully beef are distributed to troops of the Royal Naval Division in the trenches of France and Belgium.

British warships are shown here alongside the south wall of the main basin in Rosyth dockyard.

The *Warspite* was a Queen Elizabeth Class battleship, launched in March 1915. Like her sister ships, she was armed with massive 15-inch guns as well as a secondary armament of 6-inch and 3-inch weapons. By the end of the year she was serving with the 5th Battle Squadron.

Fourteen dummy ships were created and moored in the anchorage of Scapa Flow in the early part of the war. These were usually merchantmen, converted with wood and canvas to look like British capital ships and so confuse the enemy. Between October 1914 and September 1915 the *Perthshire* was disguised to look like the battleship *Vanguard*. This shows both ships, the real *Vanguard* (right) and the imitation one (left).

Coaling a battleship. Bags of crucially important fuel are winched out of the lighter, and transferred on to the deck of the warship. In the nineteenth century it was the need for ready supplies of coal that motivated the British into acquiring coaling stations across the world. When world war came in 1914, these bases had to be protected.

October

The White Funnel Fleet of P. & A. Campbell supplied many paddle steamers to act as minesweepers during the war. The *Brighton Queen*, shown here on a pre-war trip to Boulogne, was lost on 6 October when she struck a mine off the Belgian coast.

„*Prinz Adalbert" nach dem Torpedotreffer (vor Wasser.)*

Phototypie J. Bourret, Le Mans (Copyright B. Allard)

Guerre Européenne 1914. — Sous-marin Anglais (le E 8) surveillant les navires Allemands dans la mer du Nord

Above: The submarine E8, which, on 23 October, torpedoed and sank the *Prinz Adalbert* 20 miles west of Libau. British submarines had been active in the Baltic for several weeks, sinking merchantmen like the *Svionia* on the 6th of the month.

Opposite top: The hospital ship *Aberdonian*, one of many such vessels called into service during the war years.

Opposite bottom: The old armoured cruiser *Prinz Adalbert* was virtually obsolete when E8 sent her to the bottom. Nevertheless, the effect of the sinking was immediate, and orders were issued to withdraw German heavy units from the Baltic.

This unusual photograph shows a German U-boat about to enter the hollow hull of a repair ship. She will soon be lifted clear of the water for inspection and, if required, urgent repair work.

Above: A U-boat nestles safely and securely inside the 'hospital ship' for submarines.

Right: General Sir Ian Hamilton was replaced as commander of the Gallipoli forces in October. A good-natured man, he was patently unsuited and ill-equipped to bring the Gallipoli campaign to a successful conclusion. This photograph shows Hamilton with Admiral de Robeck, commander of the naval forces in the Dardanelles, shortly before the change took place.

This shows General Birdwood, commander of the Australian and New Zealand troops at Gallipoli, swimming in the Dardanelles. The only British commander opposed to any form of withdrawal from Gallipoli, Birdwood was promoted to Lt General on 28 October, and assumed command of the new Dardanelles Army – in effect, replacing Sir Ian Hamilton.

November

Kleiner Kreuzer S.M.S. „Undine."

2700 t
21-21,1 sm
Schnelligkeit
8000
Pferdest.
262 Mann

Following their October losses, the German admiralty was forced to rethink its position in the Baltic. However, before orders for German ships to withdraw from the Baltic Sea could be implemented, the Royal Navy achieved another success on 7 November when the submarine E19 spotted, tracked and then sank the German protected cruiser *Undine* off Trelleborg.

John Jellicoe, commander of the Grand Fleet, on whom the weight of his command and its immense responsibilities were already beginning to take their toll.

Admiral Scheer

Admiral Reinhard Scheer, who began the war as commander of 11th Battle Squadron of the High Seas Fleet, rose to command the more powerful units in 111th Battle Squadron and finally, in January 1916, to command the whole of the High Seas Fleet itself.

HMS *Benbow*, sister ship of the *Iron Duke*, was launched in 1914. She was yet another new ship for the Royal Navy, and served with the 4th Battle Squadron. This shows her leaving Beardmores on the Clyde.

The Battle of Ctesiphon began in November 1915, part of the British campaign in Mesopotamia. It was a badly handled affair that saw the British forces retreat to the town of Kut, where they were besieged and, eventually, starved out. This shows the river gunboat *Firefly*, which, along with her sister ship *Comet*, was involved in the early stages of the battle. The gunboats *Shaitan* and *Sumani* were both lost during the campaign.

A naval brigade, shown here assembled in line. Units of the various naval brigades and the Royal Marines continued to be used throughout the war.

An unusual photograph showing bombs made from torpedo warheads on board HMS *Agamemnon*.

Members of the crew of the light cruiser *Bristol* are shown here on the deck of their ship, in West Africa, in around 1915.

Despite the war, the fishing industry continued to operate. Some trawlers were requisitioned, some captains and crewmen were called away to serve in the Navy, but providing fish for the table remained a vitally important part of the war effort. Here, girls can be seen gutting herring. They also did jobs that only a few years before were the preserve of the men.

A German U-boat crew is seen here on the deck of their boat. Conditions inside the U-boats were not good and men took every opportunity to grab fresh air whenever they could – always keeping a wary eye out for airships or scouting sea planes.

Destroyers were constantly on patrol, searching for lurking U-boats. This shows the *Mohawk* in heavy seas – whatever the weather, the hunt had to go on.

December

H.M.S. "Thames.

The *Thames* was built at Pembroke dockyard as a cruiser. Despite an accident soon after her launch, when a small yacht was dragged under by the suction from her propellers, the *Thames* was a long-serving vessel, and was converted into a submarine depot ship at the beginning of the twentieth century. This view shows her off Essex during the early war years.

German capital ships may have been pulled out of the Baltic but other units remained. On 17 December the cruiser *Bremen*, along with the destroyer V191, was sunk by the submarine E9. This artist-drawn view shows the *Bremen* before the disaster.

Armoured cars of the Royal Naval Division are shown here at Gallipoli, the RND fighting to the end.

A postcard from the RND, sent from overseas.

As 1915 drew to a close, the submarine war continued, as brutal and as cruel as ever. This shows British merchant seamen clinging to the hull of their lifeboat. In what was a ridiculous and uncaring procedure, the wages of merchant seamen were stopped the moment their ship was sunk, often leaving their families destitute, without means of support.

The E13 had gone ashore on the Danish coast in August 1915, and the helpless craft was attacked by German motorboats, her crew machine-gunned in the water. It was a major diplomatic incident, as the German attack took place in neutral waters. After a few months, the Danish Navy raised the E13 (shown here), but the damage was too severe and the wreck was scrapped.

The RNAS pilot Commander Charles Samson had already made a name for himself in August 1914. Now, on 18 December 1915 he flew his aircraft over the Turkish forces on the Dardanelles and dropped a 500-lb bomb on them – the largest explosive device yet dropped by an aircraft. This shows Samson's floatplane on the water.

The Gallipoli landings had resulted in major losses, of both ships and men. Vessels like the *Irresistible*, shown here sinking in the Dardanelles, were hard to replace. When Lord Kitchener visited the area in the autumn of 1915 he was adamant that the beaches would have to be evacuated. The Government reluctantly agreed.

The evacuation of the Anzac and Suvla beachheads began on 19 December, most of the men being taken off in small boats, trawlers and drifters, as shown here. The full evacuation was largely completed by 21 December, and was hugely successful. The Turks did not realise the men were gone until it was too late to interfere with the operation.

The steam picket boat of a British cruiser. Vessels like this were used to pick up soldiers from the Gallipoli beaches.

The Gallipoli campaign might be over, but on 23 December naval operations began on Lake Tanganika in East Africa – yet another front opening up. The war on this huge inland lake did not involve capital ships, just launches and small boats like the one shown here, but it was fought with equal intensity by both sides.

A German gun crew at work on the deck of their launch/gunboat, December 1915. British success was immediate, with Kingani captured on Boxing Day 1915.

The Dover Patrol became increasingly important, its destroyers, monitors and airships guarding against German attacks by submarines and surface vessels. This shows trawlers and drifters from the patrol out in the Channel, on a sweep for mines.

The destroyer HMS *Swift*, part of the Dover Patrol.

HMS *Wisteria*, a minesweeper belonging to the new Flower Class of sloops first commissioned in 1914, is shown here in rough seas – a miserable existence for everyone concerned.

Opposite bottom: British Red Cross nurses arrive at Dieppe, lining the side of their transport ship in excitement. Within days they would be experiencing the horrors of the front line.

hey grew in beauty side by side
On Billy's upper lip,
ill Tommy Atkins cut them off—
Now Billy's got the pip.

Another patriotic card, this time showing the Kaiser having his moustache clipped by hardy British warriors!

Opposite top: A close up view of the 6-inch guns on HMS *Changuinola*.

Opposite bottom: Coffins of the *Lusitania* victims make a poignant picture, which brings home the hideous nature of war.

The German battlecruiser *Derfflinger*. With 1915 drawing to a close, the threat of the German High Seas Fleet had not been eliminated, merely restrained. It remained a strong, powerful and potent threat.

The *Baden*, with her powerful 15-inch main armament, was just one cause for British concern. A reckoning was surely coming; it was just a matter of working out when.

The year 1915 ended with disaster when the armoured cruiser *Natal* suddenly blew up in a sheet of flame on the afternoon of New Year's Eve 1915. Anchored in the Cromarty Firth, the ship seemed safe in port, and everyone was enjoying the Christmas and New Year celebrations. Then came disaster.

People on the *Natal* simply did not know what was happening as a series of explosions rocked the ship. A total of 404 sailors were lost, along with seven women and three children, who had been invited on board to watch a film show. At first it was thought the ship had been struck by a torpedo, but divers, sent down to investigate the wreck, discovered she had been destroyed by internal explosions, probably caused by faulty cordite.

As the year ended, it was clear that the war would go on for some time. The battle fleets of Germany and Britain had not come to blows, but the U-boat menace was growing.